4/05

Peyton Manning

By Jeff Savage

AMAZING ATHLETES

LERNER**SPORTS** / Minneapolis

This book is available in two editions:
Library binding by LernerSports
Soft cover by First Avenue Editions
Imprints of Lerner Publishing Group
241 First Avenue North
Minneapolis, MN 55401 U.S.A.

Website address: www.lernerbooks.com

Library of Congress Cataloging-in-Publication Data

Savage, Jeff
    Peyton Manning / by Jeff Savage.
        p.   cm. – (Amazing athletes)
    Includes index.
    ISBN: 0–8225–4034–7 (lib. bdg. : alk. paper)
    ISBN: 0–8225–2524–0 (pbk. : alk. paper)
    1. Manning, Peyton—Juvenile literature. 2. Football players—United States—Biography—
Juvenile literature. I. Title. II. Series.
    GV939.M289S27 2005
    796.332'092—dc22   2004005805

Manufactured in the United States of America
1 2 3 4 5 6 – JR – 10 09 08 07 06 05

TABLE OF CONTENTS

Peyton Manning prepares to pass during the 2003
game against the Tampa Bay Buccaneers.

A CALM WINNER

The clock was ticking as Indianapolis
quarterback Peyton Manning got ready to pass.
Fewer than four minutes were left in this 2003
Monday Night Football game.

The Indianapolis Colts were down 35–14
against the Super Bowl champions, the Tampa

Bay Buccaneers. No team in National Football League (NFL) history had ever won when trailing by so many points with so little time left.

Members of the Bucs **defense** swarmed all around Peyton. He passed the ball to teammate Troy Walters, who gained six yards. On the next play, Peyton handed the ball to James Mungro, who plunged into the **end zone** for a **touchdown**. Score!

The Bucs defense tries to stop Peyton and his team from scoring.

Peyton has almost total control of the game. Peyton's coach, Tony Dungy, lets Petyon change the plays on the field.

But did the touchdown come too late? Peyton's Indianapolis Colts were behind by two touchdowns, and time was running out. The Tampa Bay Buccaneers had the best defense in football. The Bucs fans were screaming for a win.

Peyton stayed calm. When the Colts got the ball back, Peyton led them down the field again. He fired a 28-yard pass to Marvin Harrison for a touchdown. Suddenly, the Colts only were

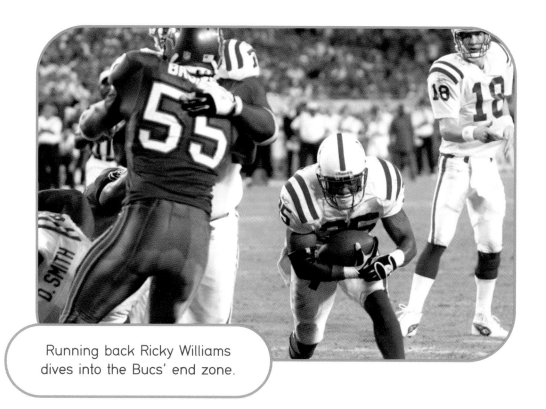

Running back Ricky Williams dives into the Bucs' end zone.

behind, 35–28. They needed just one more touchdown and extra point to tie the game!

Tampa Bay tried to use up all the time on the clock. The Colts' defense got tough and got back the ball. Peyton had one chance to tie the game. The Colts marched toward the **goal line.** With 35 seconds left, Ricky Williams dived into the end zone. With the kick after, the game was tied!

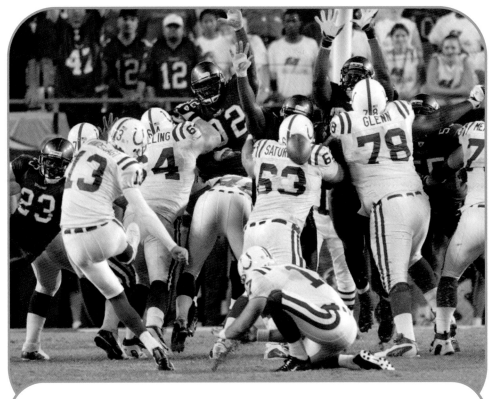

Facing the Bucs defense, Mike Vanderjagt *(wearing number 13)* kicks the overtime field goal that wins the game for the Colts.

But the game wasn't over yet. The teams went into **overtime.** The first team to score would win. Peyton guided his team to the Tampa Bay 11-yard line. From there, Colts' kicker Mike Vanderjagt successfully booted a **field goal.**

The Colts broke into a wild celebration. They had refused to give up, and their reward was a stunning 38–35 victory. "Sometimes it's hard to keep believing," Peyton said, "but I never lost confidence."

October 6 was also Coach Dungy's birthday. What a birthday present!

Coach Dungy and Peyton celebrate the victory on October 6, 2003.

Peyton's parents—Archie Manning and Olivia Williams—both went to the University of Mississippi. The school is nicknamed Ole Miss.

BORN TO THROW

Peyton Williams Manning was born March 24, 1976, to Archie and Olivia Manning. Olivia had been the homecoming queen at the University of Mississippi, where Archie had also been a star player. Archie had been an NFL quarterback for fourteen years, playing mostly for the New Orleans Saints.

Peyton and his brothers—Cooper and Eli—lived with their parents in New Orleans, Louisiana. They often watched their father play.

Archie *(running with ball)* played for the New Orleans Saints for twelve years. Even though Archie played well, the team wasn't very good during his career.

Peyton loved football from the start. By age three, he was playing the game with his father and older brother, Cooper, in the living room. Archie would carry a tiny football and try to scoot past his boys on his knees. By age four, Peyton was throwing his little football perfectly. Each Christmas, Peyton and his brothers would find gifts of helmets, jerseys, and other football gear beneath their tree. Peyton dreamed of someday being a quarterback, just like his dad.

Peyton went to Isidore Newman School from kindergarten through high school and earned good grades. In 1991, he became the quarterback for the school's **varsity** team. Cooper

Cooper Manning got a serious disease just before he started college. He was to play football for Ole Miss. The surgery he had to have ended his football career.

Peyton had dreamed of being at Ole Miss with his brother Cooper. When that dream came apart, he decided to start fresh at the University of Tennessee.

was his favorite **wide receiver.** Before Peyton got the ball, he'd make secret hand signals to his brother. Cooper knew exactly where to run, and Peyton would throw him the ball.

Peyton played quarterback for the varsity for three years. During that time, he led Isidore Newman to thirty-five wins and just five losses. Many colleges wanted Peyton to play football for their teams. He picked the University of Tennessee in Knoxville.

Peyton deeply respected his father *(right)*. He wanted to live up to Archie's college success.

STUDENT OF THE GAME

Peyton was proud to wear the orange-and-white uniform of the Tennessee Volunteers. In 1994, as a freshman, he was the **third-string** quarterback. Even though he didn't play yet, he practiced hard. He wanted to be ready to play if the team needed him. Peyton was needed sooner than anyone expected.

In the first game of the season, the first-string, or starting, quarterback got hurt. Two weeks later, the second-string quarterback got hurt too. Suddenly, Peyton was the team's quarterback.

Peyton was named the starting quarterback in his first year at the University of Tennessee.

Peyton worked hard to learn the plays that would bring his team victory.

In his first game, he was careful not to throw an **interception.** The Volunteers won, 10–9. Peyton grew more confident. He led his team to six wins in its last seven games. He even guided the Volunteers to a 45–23 win over Virginia Tech in the Gator Bowl.

Peyton was a serious college student who earned good grades. He also studied the football team's **playbook** and looked at **game films.** Peyton's hard work paid off. In the 1995 season, he set team records for **completions** and yards passing. The University of Tennessee was named one of the best teams in the country.

Tennessee head coach Phillip Fulmer *(left)* worked with Peyton throughout his time at the University of Tennessee.

By 1996, Peyton had become a statewide hero. When people saw him at restaurants or malls, they chanted his name. The town of Knoxville, Tennessee, named a street Peyton Manning Pass. Peyton was uncomfortable with all the fuss. In 1997, his senior season, he led the Volunteers to an 11–1 record. They earned the right to play in the Orange Bowl.

College bowl games take place after the regular season is over. They show off the country's best teams.

Peyton holds up the jersey of the Indianapolis Colts, the team that drafted him in 1998.

ALL-PRO THROWER

Peyton knew he wanted to play in the NFL after he finished college in 1998. Many football experts thought he was sure to be one of the first players chosen in the 1998 NFL **Draft.** The Indianapolis Colts had the first pick, and they chose Peyton.

The Colts offered Peyton a **contract** for $48 million to play for them for six years. Peyton agreed and immediately set up the PeyBack Foundation. This group would give money to people in need.

But Peyton had a big job ahead. The Colts were losers. They had won just three of sixteen games in the 1997 season. Most **rookie** quarterbacks don't play in their first year, but the Colts really needed Peyton's help.

Peyton's first season was tough. Here, he's getting tackled by a member of the New York Jets.

At training camp, before the start of his second season, Peyton ran sprints to become faster and more fit.

He struggled, winning just three games in the 1998 season. "It was frustrating," Peyton said. "But you can either sit there and feel sorry for yourself or learn from it and do something about it."

Peyton worked harder than ever to get himself ready for the 1999 season. He lifted weights and ran sprints. He memorized the team playbook—not just the plays for the quarterback but every play in the book. Could he help his team be a winner?

Peyton studied hard to learn the Colts' playbook. Soon his coaches trusted him to change plays on the field.

Peyton focused on playing well in the 1999 season. He turned the Colts into winners. Indianapolis's 13–3 record was the biggest improvement in NFL history. Six of the wins were fourth-quarter **comebacks,** showing that

Peyton was calm in the final minutes. The Colts even made it to the NFL **playoffs** but lost the first playoff game.

They won ten games in the 2000 season to reach the playoffs again. Unfortunately, they lost again. The Colts had a worse season in 2001, with six wins and ten losses. In the 2002 season, Peyton's team reached the postseason yet again. This time, the Colts were crushed 41–0 by the New York Jets. Some people wondered if Peyton could win in the playoffs.

Peyton and Steve McNair *(left)* shared Most Valuable Player honors for the 2003 season.

ALL THE RIGHT MOVES

The Colts won twelve games in 2003 to make the playoffs again. Peyton was named the NFL's co-Most Valuable Player (MVP). He shared the honor with Steve McNair, the quarterback of the Tennessee Titans.

On January 4, 2004, nearly 60,000 Colts fans filled the RCA Dome in Indianapolis. They wanted to see if Peyton could win a playoff game. Peyton made all the right moves. He passed for a whopping 377 yards and five touchdowns to lead his team to a 41–10 defeat of the Denver Broncos. "It feels good to get that first one," Peyton said afterward.

The Colts won their first playoff game in 2004. They beat the Denver Broncos in front of an excited Colts crowd.

> The Colts had a great win against the Kansas City Chiefs. Peyton threw for 304 yards and three touchdowns.

The following week, Peyton torched the Kansas City Chiefs for 304 yards and three touchdowns in a 38–31 victory. The Colts' season ended when the New England Patriots beat them, 24–14.

> The Patriots went on to win the Super Bowl.

The Colts rewarded Peyton for his incredible play with a new contract. He was to be paid

$99 million over the next seven years. Peyton was also chosen to go to the Pro Bowl. This game features the best NFL players.

The even bigger contract didn't lessen Peyton's interest in giving back to his community. He and his wife Ashley care deeply about all children. His foundation gives hundreds of thousands of dollars every year to Toys for Tots and Boys and Girls Clubs.

Peyton joined Steve McNair *(left)* and Trent Green *(center)* at the Pro Bowl.

Peyton and Eli Manning stand on either side of their father. Eli played quarterback at Ole Miss. He was the first pick in the 2004 NFL Draft and plays for the New York Giants.

"I try to be a person that people can look up to," Peyton says. "I'm not doing it for any fake reasons. That's the person I want to be. My parents taught me to do the right thing, and that's what I try to do."

Selected Career Highlights

2004 Named NFL Quarterback of the Year by National
Quarterback Club
Won ESPY award as Best NFL Player

2003 Named NFL co-MVP
Named NFL Player of the Year by Maxwell
Football Club
Set NFL record for throwing at least twenty-
five touchdown passes in six straight seasons
Selected to Pro Bowl for fourth time

2002 Selected to Pro Bowl for third time

2001 Led the American Football Conference (AFC) in passing yards

2000 Broke team record for touchdown passes in a season, with
thirty-three
Became fifth quarterback in NFL history to pass for over 4,000
yards in a season
Selected to Pro Bowl for second time

1999 Selected to Pro Bowl for first time

1998 Selected first in the NFL draft

1997 Won the Sullivan Award, given each year to the nation's top
amateur athlete
Selected Associated Press first team All-America
Finished college career with thirty-three school records and two
NCAA records

1996 Selected Associated Press third team All-America
Became first Tennessee quarterback to pass for more than 3,000
yards in a season

1995 Selected Associated Press third team All-America
Set an NCAA record for lowest interception rate in a season

1994 Named Southeastern Conference Freshman of the Year

Glossary

comeback: a win in the final minutes of a game after a team has been losing

completion: the catch of a pass from the quaterback

contract: a written deal signed by a player and his or her team. The player agrees to play for the team for a stated number of years. The team agrees to pay the player a stated amount of money.

defense: the team of eleven players that doesn't have the football. The defense tries to stop the other team from scoring.

draft: a yearly event in which all professional teams in a sport are given the chance to pick new players from a selected group

end zone: the area beyond the goal line. To score, a team tries to get the ball into the other team's end zone.

field goal: a successful kick over the U-shaped upright poles. A field goal is worth three points.

game film: a videotape of a game that players and coaches can study

goal line: the line at the edge of the end zone that a team crosses to score points

interception: a pass that is caught by a person on the defense. An interception results in the opposing team getting control of the ball.

overtime: in NFL rules, an extra fifteen minutes played when opposing football teams are tied. The first team to score wins.

playbook: a book that describes plays a team will use in games

playoffs: a series of games played after the regular season has ended

rookie: a player who is playing his or her first season

third-string: the name given to the third player at a certain position. The first-string player is the starting player. The second-string player replaces the first-string player and so on.

touchdown: a score in which the team with the ball crosses its opponent's goal line. A touchdown is worth six points.

varsity: the school team made up of the most experienced or best players

wide receiver: a player who catches passes, mainly for a big gain

Further Reading & Websites

Hyams, Jimmy. *Peyton Manning: Primed and Ready.* Shawnee Mission, KS: Addax Publishing Group, 1998.

Manning, Peyton, and Archie Manning. *Manning: A Father, His Sons and a Football Legacy.* New York: HarperEntertainment, 2000.

Rappoport, Ken. *Super Sports Star Peyton Manning.* Berkeley Heights, NJ: Enslow Publishers, Inc., 2003.

Savage, Jeff. *Peyton Manning: Precision Passer.* Minneapolis: LernerSports, 2001.

Stewart, Mark. *Peyton Manning: Rising Son.* Brookfield, CT: Millbrook Press, 2000.

Wilner, Barry. *Peyton Manning.* Berkeley Heights, NJ: Enslow Publishers, Inc., 2003.

Official NFL Site
<http://www.nfl.com>
The official National Football League website that provides fans with game action, biographies of players, and information about football.

Peyton's Website
<http://www.peytonmanning.com>
Peyton's official website, featuring trivia, photos, and information about Peyton and his PeyBack Foundation.

Sports Illustrated for Kids
<http://www.sikids.com>
The *Sports Illustrated for Kids* website that covers all sports, including football.

Index

Photo Acknowledgments

Photographs are used with the permission of: © SportsChrome East/West, Rob Tringali, pp. 4, 29; © Charles W. Luzier/Reuters/CORBIS, pp. 5, 9; © Eliot J. Schechter/Getty Images, p. 6; © AP/Wide World Photos, pp. 7, 27; © Pierre DuCharme/Reuters/CORBIS, p. 8; © University of Mississippi, p. 10; © Bettmann/CORBIS, p. 11; © The University of Tennessee, pp. 13, 16; © Jamie Squire/Getty Images, pp. 14, 19; © Jonathan Daniel/Getty Images, p. 15; © Reuters/CORBIS, pp. 17, 22; © Al Bello/Getty Images, p. 20; © Brent Smith/Reuters/Getty Images, p. 21; © Ronald Martinez/Getty Images, p. 24; © Donald Miralle/Getty Images, p. 25; © Mike Blake/Reuters/CORBIS, p. 26; © Icon SMI, p. 28.

Cover: © SportsChrome East/West, Michael Zito.